M000074458

Sunday Evening at

The Stardust Café

For Phyllys,
with gratitude
and love.

Wb
3/1/07

Poems by

W. E. BUTTS

W. C. Butts

1st WORLD
PUBLISHING

Sunday Evening at the Stardust Café

W. E. BUTTS

Winner of the Iowa Source Poetry Book Prize

© W. E. Butts 2006

Published by 1stWorld Publishing
1100 North 4th St. Suite 131, Fairfield, Iowa 52556
tel: 641-209-5000 • fax: 641-209-3001
web: www.1stworldpublishing.com

First Edition

LCCN: 2006901412
SoftCover ISBN: 1-59540-829-0
HardCover ISBN: 1-59540-831-2
eBook ISBN: 1-59540-830-4

All rights reserved. No part of this book may be reproduced or utilized in any form or by any means, electronic or mechanical, including photocopying or recording, or by any information storage and retrieval system, without permission in writing from the author.

This material has been written and published solely for educational purposes. The author and the publisher shall have neither liability or responsibility to any person or entity with respect to any loss, damage or injury caused or alleged to be caused directly or indirectly by the information contained in this book.

The characters and events described in this text are intended to entertain and teach rather than present an exact factual history of real people or events.

Cover art: James de Crescentis, *"Falling through the Net with Waves"* (acrylic and ink on paper)

Acknowledgments

Grateful acknowledgment is made to the following publications where these poems first appeared, sometimes in different versions:

The Acre: "Serial"
American Poets & Poetry: "Monarch"
Atlanta Review: "Nocturne"
The Aurora: "Eight Ball"; "My Father's Name"
Café Review: "Toward Winter"
Calliope: "Innocence"; "1954: Two Parades"
Cider Press Review: "All Our Quick Days"; "Invocation"
The Contemporary Review: "Black Squirrels"; "Selling the Church"; "Smoke"; "The Station"
Defined Providence: "Particular Hearts"
Fact of the Universe: "At the Merrimack"; "Seaport"
The Iowa Source: "The Note"
Maelstrom: "Mountain of Love"
Mid-American Review: "Cobalt"; "Communal"; "Prelude"; "September"; "Sunday Evening at the Stardust Café"
Pine Island Journal: "Chances"
Poet Lore: "Against Desire"; "Magic Acts"; "The Necktie"
Poetry East: "Predictions"
Rhino: "The Blessing"
Slant: "A Brief History"
Spillway: "A Chronology of Birds"; "Arboretum"; "The Messengers"
Two Rivers Review: "Observance"

"City That Never Sleeps," "Clay Street," "The Question," "Sunday Factory," and "The Train" were first published in a chapbook, *Sunday Factory,* from Finishing Line Press.

Some of the poems in this collection were reprinted in *Movies in a Small Town* (Mellen Poetry Press, 1997), *A Season of Crows* (Igneus Press, 2000), *White Bees* (Oyster River Press, 2001), and *Sunday Factory* (Finishing Line Press, 2006). My thanks to the editors.

Many thanks to Tom Absher, David Allan Evans, James Haug, and Jack Myers, whose comments and advice helped shape this book, and with gratitude to Rustin Larson.

I also wish to express my deep appreciation to James de Crescentis, William Kemmett, Peter Kidd, Keith Kuzmak, and Richard Martin for their friendship and the collective sustaining spirit that exists in many of these poems.

for Stephanie

Contents

I. One Day in the Fifties

September

I wonder what it means to think of certain people
after years of forgetting.
You're doing nothing, then suddenly
there is your uncle with a club foot
and crippled hand, who loved sports
and wrote histories for children,
your father who shot the eyes off pool balls,
your boyhood friend who closed himself
inside the garage, motor running,
and went to sleep. I know a man who painted
his town the color of distant hills,
so stepping inside its shops and offices
was like entering a field of mint
or passing under forest light.
This month, on a calendar above the desk,
Japanese warlords have closed the bridge,
and the people must turn away from their temple.
There are times I've thought I was going to die,
but didn't. Tonight I'm here beneath the swords
that threaten to slice off the heads of faith.
There is a blue circle around the date of my birth.
I remember a woman who collected her past
like pieces of shell from the sand.
I remember those glass beads of prayer
dangling from my mother's arthritic fingers.
I remember the ragman, carriage, and horse,

peddling his iron and cloth. I think of a saint
who wore burlap, and spoke with rabbit and sparrow.
I know a man who listens to the hours
trapped in the throats of tiny wooden birds.
It's hard to tell from here, where the white bees
of my body have gathered, if memory
is sacrament or penance.

A Chronology of Birds

1951. Bored with magic shows
and lemonade stands, we needed
some deeper ceremony,
so when we found the crushed sparrow
by the roadside we stared
awhile, poked its body
with sticks, trembled a little
in our seven-year-old fascination.

Then I remembered Father's harmonica,
ran to the house and took it
from its shiny metal case.
Up and down the small town's street,
our procession of children marched;
one boy carrying the bird
and its death stench
on a small slab of bark.

I pressed my tongue to each fret,
blew, but made the wrong sound,
a dirge—not that first language
of breath, song, and trill.
Meanwhile, there were birds
collecting in the trees.
We could only answer them
with silence.

Innocence

I'm dressed inside the family album
for First Communion, pushing my tongue
against the fleshy space where a tooth had been,
and I love Mother and Father, Jesus
and the Blessed Virgin,
a girl in my second grade class
who yells at me for following her.
Look, I'm nearly forgivable
standing under a chorus of angels
in this white suit, even though
once, while reading aloud from *Black Beauty*,
I declared that horse's coat
to be "smooth as Satan,"
and so was held back a year
because, as the nun explained
later to my shamed parents,
I was a strange boy who could not read.

There's a fast-food restaurant
in place of the dining car
where Mother worked, photographs
of it framed in plastic on the wall.
And I remember a trucker
who promised me cowboy boots and hat,
but never drove through town again,
summers on the front porch
watching the Thruway being built,

W. E. Butts

reports of traffic fatalities
in the local gazette, my father
telling stories to the neighborhood kids,
making each, in turn, a hero,
six-guns drawn, riding a sleek stallion.

I would save us all now, if I could,
from the herd of mistakes
galloping through our hearts.
Once, reshaping our lives
was an easy ritual of customized cars,
rolled-up sleeves, and petroleum jelly.
Then we left town,
or punched in at the factory.
Nothing was simple. No one was blameless.

One Day in the Fifties

We returned from factory shift,
dining car dishes, childhood's river
and flow—Father, Mother, and I—
where our routines were small prayers
offered to that god of simple requests,
who would bless each day
for what it was worth.

Television reported
one of its many events,
and a nervous eyewitness
described the car leaving
the road near the bridge,
its crazy swerve down the bank,
its crash into willow.

Thank God, Mother said,
it was no one
we knew. It was time
for the variety show, and a thin man
hurried across the stage,
balancing spinning plates
on long poles from his forehead
and extended arms,
two tiny white poodles
yapping at his ankles,
and all of us laughed.

W. E. Butts

1954: Two Parades

Just home from Korea, a decorated war hero was leaning
toward the crowd, from the hotel's third floor,
and we heard the drum roll, marching band,
rifle-fire in the humid air, Mother and I,
while Father worked the late shift.

Didn't I know what war was,
times in the weeds I waited for the enemy?
Little Bobby lost an eye in one of those battles,
shot out by his own brother's pellet gun.
I remember, all those childhood years after,
his glass-marble stare seemed wrong,
and his brother's self-hatred.

That was the summer the daughter of the kind woman
who owned the dining car my mother washed dishes in
became Miss New York State, in a parade of lace
and lilacs, their petals the pale lavender
of a heart on the breast of a graceless uniform,
or the satin that ten years later would line my father's casket.
We all stood cheering on the street
to wave along the beauty we were not.

Serial

One afternoon, while we waited
for the Saturday matinee, a pick-up truck
moved slowly down Main Street,
and Mighty Joe Young,
the gorilla hero, stood
on the flatbed
waving his arms by remote control,
eyes lit and flashing
like small red bulbs in a bowtie
I won in fifth grade,
for selling the most magazines.
Weeks I sat in the back
of the classroom,
stoical as a confirmed bachelor.

Again and again, I pushed the button
of that battery in my pocket,
hoping some girl would notice.
I wanted to be Mighty Joe Young,
and break out of the cage of inadequacy
built by years of parochial school
and atomic power.
It wouldn't matter then
if I looked like an ape,
scratched myself,
or got beat up by the older kids.
I would always be taking

the beautiful woman
away to the rainforest.

This was around the same time
I noticed the theater
manager's twelve-year-old daughter,
and her long hair
streaming over her shoulders
like the light
that so often swirled above my head
toward the movie screen,
and all I really knew of love.
Even now, I feel
like someone from an audience
installed in the electricity
of future events.

Mountain of Love

Saturday nights, we skated
to rock and roll music,
and weaved around girls.
In our songs
there was always someone
who needed love,
and would, like us,
do almost anything to get it.

That year,
we wore fluorescent pants
with a buckle on the back,
carefully folded sleeves
and slicked hair,
laced our boots half-way,
and spun on full-precision
wooden wheels, each turn
waiting like a first date.

Rhythms of Duane Eddy
and Johnny Rivers
propelled us through games
of whip and chicken,
where danger could be played
inside the wings of our collars,
each of us knowing
he'd circle back
to join the others.

W. E. Butts

It was not like now,
coming home from your job
on second shift,
your body aching
in ways it never did
at seventeen,
and you keep repeating
the wrong words
to some half-remembered lyric—
not from love, but need—
until you can almost believe
you are loosened
from that snapping line
your life has been.

Black Squirrels

(A Gathering of Poets, Kent State University, May, 1990)

Field after field, and gray sky.
Two days on the road, and we're here
for the gathering. After the shootings,
as students drove away from Kent State,
townspeople sat quietly on their porches,
some of them holding rifles.
Back then, like everyone else I knew,
I was going to parties. Once, at one of them,
after I'd taken a hit of blotter acid,
I stared at the bathroom mirror
and it was me all right, only forty years older.
I remember how I went about that evening
with my white hair and beard, my weathered skin,
considerably less astonished by my transformation
than Kafka's Gregor. Our brains were filled
with tiny windows we had to look through.
That's why I was screaming over the bloodied corpse
lying in some Vietnamese field,
or raging against Attica's injustice,
arguing with my parents in the Philco's flickering light.
Everywhere, in May, 1970, the shocked "O"
of that girl on the hill was circling around us.
Twenty years later, poets have come
to read lyrics and remember.
I'm standing next to a grotesque
abstract metal sculpture with a small hole in it,

W. E. Butts

the scream transfixed, the bullet plummeting
from its high arc above my head.
Black squirrels scurry across the quad.
The poets are still reading, their voices
accumulating into songs, like those
of the bright canaries that, a century ago,
led coal miners who lived here
in and out of their darkness.

A Brief History

Anything is enough if you know how poor you are.
You could step out now in wonder.

—Larry Levis

We danced with older women
wearing beehive hairdos,
1975, New Year's Eve,
in a country-western bar—
danced as if we could not die.
I look at the mirror's creased face.
All this time,
I've been shadowed by mistake.
Was it wrong to stay poor?
On bad days, we threw the I Ching,
and meditated for money.
There were some drugged evenings
candles could explode
in front of us,
and we would not care.
It seemed like everyone else
was hurriedly driving
toward their unfinished work,
past the burnt-out buildings,
the morning's minor accidents.

W. E. Butts

Today, things are different.
They don't make acid like they used to,
my friend reminds me on the phone.
Why once, we even taught the dog
to talk—simple requests for food
and comfort, more music, the kind
you'd die for, like Joplin and Hendrix.
Back then, it was easy lying together,
the world so liquid and strange.
But now, most often, night after night,
our bodies bargain desire.
It's not enough anymore,
to watch the neon flickering
inside our brains,
to be surrounded by the vaporous
aura of everything.
Like my friend says,
we opened the door, so now
we are here, wondering.

The Note

Like when you're inside a shopping mall,
I listen to birds chattering,
a kind of background music
you get used to,
but their song makes me strangely sad,
the way the extraordinarily beautiful
always will.
A teenager sits alone with a trumpet
on the top row of bleachers
at the edge of an empty football field,
his instrument returning his breath
with tuneless bursts.
He is like someone giving mouth-to-mouth
to the nearly drowned,
as I was years ago,
before I broke through the creek's surface,
and entered the world's loud opera.
That was the same place
my father and two uncles learned to swim,
when Grandfather tossed them in.
How often I watched
Father's sequined concert
of body and water—silence.
My father played the violin
so badly when I was a small child,
if he took it out of the case,

W. E. Butts

I would scream uncontrollably.
Sometimes, the way we live
is a crazy orchestra
that we've all joined,
playing to beat the band.
But here's this kid,
who only requires the joy
of one sweet note,
and will try again and again,
until whatever it is he feels
can be finally lifted
into the brightness of voices and wings.

Sunday Evening at
the Stardust Café

Young people smoke cigarettes,
drink coffee, flirt. A strip of violet
neon tubing thrusts from between the breasts
of Marilyn Monroe in a black and white poster
on the wall. On the jukebox, Neil Young
sings: "Old man, look in my eyes."
Maybe I'll join them, promise to be quick
and reckless. The young blonde
with startling eyes, that seem to reflect
everything, will take me to a quiet booth
in back, where we'll smoke and talk,
as if we're really interested in the bad art
hanging next to us. I can explain then
why my life's important. I remember Marilyn,
her mascaraed, lidded eyes, Presley
censored on Sullivan, Lennon in New York
that night at the Dakota.
Why shouldn't she fall in love?

But I don't want to say too much.
For instance, I can't tell her how sad
the silver-hooped ring dangling from her nose
makes me feel, in spite of my own gold earring.
These kids look like Rimbaud, and far as I know,
they probably are. Think of it, a dozen

reincarnated Rimbauds in a greasy spoon,
pale and dressed in black, notebooks open
to pages ready to record whatever's wrong.

I remember a film, "Wild in the Streets."
The President of the United States,
a rock musician, twenty-five and aging fast,
whose platform was built on the premise
that anyone over twenty-one was suspect,
contemplates his life. In the final frame,
a ten-year-old boy faces the camera
and promises a future of bubble-gum and baseball,
but like with anything else, there's a catch.

Back at the Stardust, the waitress,
who is friendly, brings my sandwich.
An old woman mutters, squints at the menu,
and counts her change. Tourists ride
horse-drawn carriages clapping down
the brick streets, or dance on the deck
of a cruise ship entering the harbor.
The kids take their notebooks and leave.

II. Magic Acts

Chances

That poor, cloned sheep on the evening news,
old before its time;
a man, blind for thirty years,
sight restored; the infant lifted
from the incubator at the hospital ward
in Belgrade; my new marriage;
the cat rising from its primordial sleep.

Anything can happen: the wafer
of my dead mother floating like a leaf
across the late summer lawn;
crows resting on the maple
of my father's shoulder.
Who knows what to expect?

Each morning I step out to sun,
snow, rain, blizzard, or calm sea.
Here there is nothing
I can't believe.

Magic Acts

Reality is things as they are.

—Wallace Stevens

I.

"There's a jungle in this room,"
my friends' three-year-old
daughter tells me,
then disappears, returns
waving her magic wand,
and we have it:
coiled snakes and twisted vines,
prancing zebras and swinging monkeys.
The art nouveau lampshades on the ceiling
are a pair of exotic birds,
and the afternoon progresses
in amusement and delight:
a warm African wind across the veldt,
lions preening near the bushes.

II.

Some mornings,
between the bed and bathroom mirror,
I could be anybody:
a man who's learned
there's a trick to everything,
doves swirling white smoke
above his head—
a man with a rabbit
full of luck,
a routine of illusions,
the confidence
of someone who knows
exactly how all of this is done.

The Messengers

Between here
and there,
the radio tuned
to my favorite rock station,
I'm all engine and song,
my hands two birds
of determined flight.

Consider the complaint
of jay and wind,
the persistence of squirrel,
the burden of walnut,
the curse of dead leaves
on my windshield,
then the hours
of work I'm driving toward.

At each turn and stop
I wonder what it means—
this daily migration
of commuter and trucker,
schoolchild and police,
jogger and transient;
the punctuation
of blinking lights
and stalled traffic.

W. E. Butts

Tonight in the yard
with my tired eyes,
the grass wet
under my yellow leaves,
a ballet of light
dances around me,
and above my head
birds repeat
the day's small thoughts.

But, just now,
on the elm branches,
those dark mystics,
the crows,
wearing their black capes,
their heads bowed
in the sudden gray air,
tell me everything
I'll need to learn.

All Our Quick Days

I'm at it again, my old routine
of going places I don't want to be,
because this is what the world
of subways and bank accounts expects.
Overhead, silent messages
of disaster and warning flash
across a computerized screen.
Somewhere in Japan, the car I'm waiting for
was built, the stops I'll make in Boston
recorded in Chicago.
It's no wonder I'm confused.
I tell you, we're not ready for this.
Think about the masturbating monkeys
in a zoo. Years ago, someone homeless
and drunk said to me, "Desire
deferred sickens the heart."
My sick heart trembles now,
and climbs under the artificial suns
of all our quick days.
The purgatory of our troubled sleep
is why I don't take naps.
Instead, I'm sitting with a book open,
pen and paper on the table,
television sound turned off,
not really sure of what I'm doing,
and so look up at the babies being held

W. E. Butts

underwater by smiling adults
whose heads are nodding in the breathable air,
and although I can't hear an explanation,
I know it has to do with this theory
that fish, frog, infant, and corpse
are all connected,
and it's only time that separates us
from the submerged children.

City That Never Sleeps

Chill Wills, a popular character actor during the 1940's and 50's, was the voice of Francis (The Talking Mule), in the Universal Pictures series, and was cast as Chicago, the city itself, in human form in the 1953 film noir classic, "City That Never Sleeps."

—from Leonard Maltin's 2003 Movie and Video Guide

Listen. If I can play a talking mule, I can do this. Think about it. How many times did you see me handle Donald, that foolish kid who'd rather dance through the finale than go someplace quiet with the pretty girl who's put up with him the entire movie? Look. Since I was twelve, there's been a red-haired woman dancing inside my head, slowly almost removing the veils shrouding her secret places, but there's always some cop blowing the whistle, and now this: just when the gumshoe who'd been following my every thought was about to quit, he's pulled back in by that dame at the Flamingo, and I can't warn the flatfoot not to leave his wife because the el is rattling the tracks louder than gunfire. But you know how it is, to have your life fast-forwarding like a runaway train; this is just one night, and who wouldn't want a chance to be his own city.

Smoke

I'm thinking about the weightlessness
of certain things at this coffee shop:
memory, steam, regret, future.
But then there's that film
I saw last night:
a writer whose wife was killed
in a drive-by shooting
tells the story of how Sir Walter Raleigh
took a set of scales,
placed a cigar on one, the ashes
of a smoked cigar on the other,
and calculated the difference
as the weight of the human soul.
But it's hard to measure
the feelings of the characters
in that movie: the cigar store owner
who's been photographing
the same street corner every day
for more than twenty years;
the writer who, while looking at the photographs,
sees his wife, alive and crossing
the busy street;
the one-eyed wife of the store owner;
the ex-convict with a prosthetic arm;
the boy waiting on a curb
for the father he's never met.

And what about the equation
of those two small children spinning
on vinyl-covered stool seats just now?
I watch them turn, stop,
then turn again.
One says, "scissors."
The other says, "rock."
The first spins three times,
smiles, says, "paper."
The second cocks his thumb,
points a forefinger,
makes a clicking noise
and says, "You're dead."

W. E. Butts

Against Desire

From beneath hemlock and maple,
I listen to the drunk neighbors
across the street yelling
at their children again.

How often I've been in this yard
with cardinal and crow,
not far from the town square
with its gourmet shops
and jazz bars filled with tourists.

Isn't it wrong to curse the heart?

You might be standing, just now,
in the yellow light
of your window,
as someone you've never met
watches from a distant wharf.

Or you could be curled
on a park bench, homeless and waiting
for the Salvation Army
soup kitchen to open.

Some late nights I leave
the comfort of sofa,
walk across the small country
of my own life toward bed,
and it's like coming home.

That teenager sitting on the steps
holds her child, who sleeps
as the quiet dark surrounds us all.

W. E. Butts

Prelude

It's been a long winter,
now a nor'easter
blows a storm across the seacoast,
and those small creatures
that populate our yard and trees
are mostly gone.

When I think of the human
propensity for wrongdoing,
I could provide a litany
of examples:

a broken barn owl dangling
at the end of a frayed string;
the terrified slow boy
hanging desperately
onto a swinging gymnasium rope;

burning rags
piled on the junkman's cart;
the broken wings
of gravestone angels;

freezing bodies
curled on the subway grate
above the train driving
toward the shooting
at the next stop;

a man, alone,
in his room at night,
weeping into his empty hands.

I'm sitting next to the purring cat
as sleet pelts the skylight,

and we both wait
for the starved bird
to sing again.

W. E. Butts

Observance

Young girls racing
and giggling through fountains
of water sprouting
out of a lawn sprinkler.

Traffic rushing down
the narrow road toward
the intersection
and shopping mall.

The quick, ritalin-induced
pace of a neighborhood
kid walking past, talking
into his cellular phone.

This is summer in America,
the new millennium,
some desire or warning
flashing in everyone's eyes.

You've learned to live
with it, the way
a declawed cat learns
to live inside a house.

You both watch television,
as the President slips
in and out of war, and teenagers
dance around corpses.

And it's because
of nights like this
you've also learned to die
a little, without comment.

What was it the poet
said? Then you remember:
"Only the dreamer
can change the dream."

Meanwhile, an insomniac's
popped open stare looks out
from behind drawn curtains,
at the suddenly empty street.

W. E. Butts

Saturday Afternoon

Even the radio's blare can't keep me
from suddenly braking for those kids
scattering out of my driveway on rollerblades,
and I can't decide if they're a measure
of whatever innocence is left us,
or the predisposition
of a common suicidal tendency
rushing beneath the exploding sun
of this new millennium.

It's so easy to forget the arrow stuck
in the robin's throat—how that bird jerked
and spun toward its small death the summer
I was twelve—the torn flowers
and smashed windows. And the children
go freely over the street graced with light.

Seaport

The sea captain's picket fence destroyed
by teenagers wearing long, black raincoats. The eternal river
threatens to rise. Marathoners pass the funeral home
and parked hearse. Tomorrow, face painting in the square,
big band at night. A woman steps out of an upscale boutique
screaming into her cellular phone, "Let me tell you
all *my* problems." Under the Japanese crabapple
no one worries. Along the path through the garden of flowers,
there's a crisis of soft birds. And down we come to celebrate
the river, its tugboats and barges, all the departing ships.

W. E. Butts

Monarch

We're sitting here in summer green
of the back yard, like a couple
of ancient Chinese governors,
wise with drink and conversation,
when you interrupt our talk of loneliness,
bad jobs, money, lost children,
to say, "That's beautiful!"

And it is—a gold and black Monarch
waving between leaves,
underneath a young maple.
I believe this is sacred,
to witness a moment in the brief hours
of life of such a thing.

This is also a good time to speak
about passion, or contemplate
Li Po, who writes:
"One quick trip between
heaven and earth, then the dust
of ten thousand generations."

At the Merrimack

The river high against the shore,
its glittering, gunmetal gray
flows into rapids.

The children,
those makers of shoes, the women,
weavers of cotton, and the men
at their foundries are gone,

but the river still gives what it can.

Here is the bridge
where your name is returned,
and stones sing in the shadows.

You stand on the bank
in the repeating wind,

the only time there is.

W. E. Butts

Predictions

A spider,
the color of a rainstorm,
crawls over a rock.
A man
sits alone in his yard
in the gray afternoon,
watching the street
where a boy
leans over the trembling wheel
of a bicycle,
and teenagers
drive their incessant music.

The man understands
the logic of rain,
desire for balance,
urgent need
for someone to listen,
and thinks
how sometimes his life
is like one of those
television game shows
that gives you the answer,
but you have to guess
the question.

The Question

After the well-broadcasted storm,
I went outside with the citizens.
We got in our cars and drove
toward whatever the day would assign.
The sun glared across black ice and snow,
our numbed fingers gripped convenience
store coffee cups, clouded signatures
of breath rising everywhere;
we were bone-chilled and communal.

Listening to "Satisfaction"
on classic rock radio, I was thinking
about my friend in Florida—
his destroyed orange grove,
how he had learned to love
the space between things,
and now it was gone—
when a woman stepped out
from behind a parked truck,
her head turned away.
There was nothing to do now
but brake and watch
the woman slide back on her heels,
cars skidding behind me,
an alarm of horns startling
birds off the utility wires.
Then again, we were safe.

W. E. Butts

Before my friend moved,
we spent a night drinking wine,
It didn't seem like
we'd ever wanted much.
After all, hadn't we come
to accept the mysteries
of cancer and Zen;
wept for the children
gone tragically wrong;
and didn't we still whisper
the names of the saints?

One day you walk out
the door suddenly open
at the middle of your life,
and it's strange to be alone
in the uncertain light,
the question you've been asking
repeating itself, then gone.

III. Selling the Church

Journal

On a train to Chicago,
I stayed awake
all night in the club car.
I was seventeen,
enlisted in the Navy,
and knew nothing yet
of Cuba, Castro,
the C.I.A., or Vietnam.

When I returned to my village,
the factory had gone
on to Delaware,
the rail station closed,
but men still lived
under the bridge
by the crossing.
I knew I must leave.

In New York City,
I found work
as a foot messenger,
delivering packages
to elegant brownstones
in upper Manhattan.
I kept a journal,
and recorded my encounters
with professional dogwalkers.

I rode the Amtrak
to Boston,
where I was hired
by Harvard
to transcribe the poems
of Emily Dickinson,
and became dedicated
to the proper placement
of dashes.

Evenings, I walked
past the fishmarket
to the harbor
and its departing ships,
the stone and glass shadows
of the city behind me.
I was at that edge where
what happened next
would be the rest of my life,
or fog shrouding the shoreline.

But there was a woman
I met and sometimes,
late at night, in the dark,
I'd rise from our bed
and go quietly down
the stairs to sit at the table
with paper and pen,
those words that saved me
before emerging again,
under the lamplight.

W. E. Butts

Invocation

Blessed, today, are the starving birds
gathered on the winter yard.
Again, this morning, you draw up the blinds,
and again our cat leaps
on the sofa back to observe
the ritual in which it is
also participant. We're both
watching you now toss pieces of bread
into the chilled, wind-driven air
as a cloud of white-throated sparrows
suddenly converges, and to rise into this
simple gesture is all I can ask.

Eight Ball

There's a Buddha on my desk,
and he's laughing.
We of the West believe
if you rub the Buddha's belly,
good fortune is certain.
But none of this matters
tonight at the pool hall,
here with a friend—
his shrewd eye and steady hand.
Again, my shot
misses its intention,
and I'm moving inevitably
toward some final chance.

The Buddha was a gift
from my wife.
I believe she meant it
to point out the way
to be different from the self
is to be the self.

For example, the sly
yet generous-hearted manner
with which my friend approaches
the green table and stands,
for a moment,
like a Chinese monk
meditating at the edge
of a quiet field,
is exactly who he is.

He understands
what's important
is more than knowing
what will happen next;
that paying attention
is how we come to the small globe
about to spin away from us,
and call it "safe."

Cobalt

Here's an evening sky
to define the changing season,
as I drive toward the waterfront.
Earlier, at work, I was told
one of my clients is dying.
This led to a clinical discussion of how
he should die, and where, and once again
I cursed my inability to say "enough!"
I'm contemplating the sound
of foghorns at the harbor;
the drifting shadows of gulls;
the stalled, imported flowers
of the exotic garden;
the town's citizens walking through the park
in this time before the inevitable
coming of tourists and rollerbladers;
the dark wings of the heart.
Last night I said something selfish.
Although you are kind,
and will forgive me this, I'm afraid,
even after the most sincere penance,
one is never fully redeemed.
Nevertheless, I've stopped at a chic downtown shop
to buy a cobalt vase and single red rose.
Now, damnit, I'm remembering the Halloween afternoon
at the treatment center

he ran behind me like a child,
making little, harmless wind noises,
whispering, "I'm a ghost. Are you scared?"
I've forgotten when we began
collecting the blue glass,
but in our small apartment now, it's everywhere.

Particular Hearts

. . . Love allows us to walk
in the sweet music of our particular heart.

—Jack Gilbert

I walk to the edge of the pier,
where curious tourists point out
a single harbor seal, bobbing and lunging
in the cold winter water,
wet, brown fur slick as sex.
Here is where we've come to be astonished.
"This can't be happening to me,"
we say when things go wrong.
We wonder about the seal,
what it's doing down there,
imagine webbed feet propelling
the impossibly large body
with great speed, toward some inevitable,
glittering fish. This is the chain:
we devour, restore. Today
you and I argued, but when I returned
from seeing all this,
our particular hearts tapped
against a blue door, joined
in the necessary, exquisite surge
toward separate places on our sweat-soaked bedding,

W. E. Butts

a river of twisted sheets wrapped around our ankles,
our two hearts taking up a constant rhythm
inside their respective rooms.
So many things make us think of our lives.
Isn't that what love is?
Like this morning, in the trees,
when swallows became flash and trill,
and I wanted you here, to listen.

Toward Winter

I'm remembering a season of crows,
an explosion of leaves,
construction of a nest.

For some time now,
you've been tracking
the strategy of a particular squirrel,
worrying it will forget
the hazelnuts and almonds
we tossed on the fire-escape,
now that they're hidden
under hemlock and elm,
beneath tortured hydrangea.

The neighbor across the street
is drunk and yelling again.
He stands coatless,
furious in December chill,
pounding his fists on his door,
demanding the woman he beats
let him in.

W. E. Butts

I know the police will come soon,
talk to the woman,
reason with the man,
then drive away
in a flashing blue glow
toward someone else's scream.

We feed the squirrel.
We remember the crow.
We accumulate the sticks
of desire:

build them into something
we can live with.

Communal

Desire is the cold
nose of a squirrel
shoveling snow
on the fire-escape,
the turn of a sleepless lover.
Crows are black tongues
on bare branches.
Traffic is love moving
in and out of romance.
Twice a week, the parking lot
at the funeral parlor fills,
and each day the same drunk
stumbles to the corner store.

Now the bells
of the Baptist church,
the loud neighbors
and their children,
the horns of ships
in the harbor,
the gray afternoon
and late mail.
Waiting for you
to come home for dinner,
I think how we belong
to this community
of insomniacs and the dead,

W. E. Butts

and how that guy falling
toward his next six-pack
is more than a little like us,

the way he just wants
some time to forget,
and a place he can lie
inside a bottle, like a ship.
Yesterday, 2:00 a.m.,
in that film
about the Titanic,
passengers sang
as it went down
and those who would be saved
held one another
in their small boats,
and listened.

The Station

I could not help but cry.
The train, it left the station,
two lights on behind.
Well, the blue light was my blues,
the red light was my mind.

—Robert Johnson

And all the sadness you feel
is vibrating in the hands
of the musician by the window,
a line of traffic driving through
the rain-streaked light reflected
in the sheen of his guitar,
and that locomotive, his heart,
traveling farther
than it should have gone,
is suddenly derailed.

Earlier tonight, in a cold rain,
a man sat on the sidewalk
in front of a shop.
You tell the woman
you're with it's all right—
someone will take care of him.

W. E. Butts

So now the musician is clutching his chest.
His large, gleaming body
staggers and bends forward,
conversations at the tables
fade like the last notes of a song.

The bass player brings him water,
he swallows the pill
he's removed from his pocket,
and it's like everyone
in the room is only alive
to hear him.
The drummer with the snakeskin hatband
lays down his sticks
like a shaman laying down bones,
until the man whose heart
will always hurt can begin again.

Nocturne

What is the universe
comprised of, if not this
neighborhood, its fixed place
in things, like some star
we've been looking at our whole lives;
small satellites of birds
attending the possibility of weather;
one birdsong becoming another,
like an accumulation of light
from many stars;
the arrival, every Friday,
of a single rose
at the coffee table;
the cosmic clink
of bottles and cans
collected in the shopping carts
of sadness and hope
the homeless drive through the dark
each week;
the incredible black hole
of all our feelings?
And I'm thinking how,
in the quiet

W. E. Butts

after a late evening meal,
I watched your fingers move
in slow circles around the rim
of an empty wine glass,
which sang,
just then, like a galaxy.

Selling the Church

The cold river behind me,
I walked home through a light falling of snow
and epiphany of wind,
past a blessing of Baptist church bells,
and thought how, when I was a boy,
houses of faith seemed eternal
as the soul we children knew
would someday rise from our shocked eyes.
But what did we know then about salvation?
That first year of marriage, I came to understand
my father, who each Sunday knelt in a pew
at Mother's church, although it was a place
he had no faith in. Months later, again
at the church on my street, I'm remembering this
as I read the realtor's sign: "Sale Pending."
Between maple and pine, birds cross
in a religion of weather. What we believe to be true
is what the caretaker raking the leaves
of the minister's yard suddenly says to me:
"Snow tonight. Frost on t.v."
It's the gray river and waves against wharf pilings;
the harsh cries of circling gulls and the harbor's silence;
the ritual of a pouring of wine and quiet speech
that is our desire, our prayer.

W. E. Butts

IV. Sunday Factory

The Necktie

Father wore a necktie, third shift,
cleaning machines at the factory, blue fabric
shimmering like a summer night on the drab gray
cotton twill uniform of common deed.
Often, since then, I've tied his double Windsor,
dressing for funerals, a wedding, dinner,
some occasion involving a dark room, wine, good jazz.

I've been looking at this photograph of you and me
celebrating my last birthday at that Italian restaurant
we enjoy so much, yet hardly go to anymore,
now that we have a routine of monthly bills and simple utility.
But I'm thinking how light flashed like a star in the fingers
of the waitress who took the Polaroid shot
I'm holding, how genuine her happiness
seemed at what we all waited for,
how his smooth hand-over-hand motion
had perfectly drawn the floral-print knot.

Arboretum

The sun is a tumor
threatening our conversation.
Just now we're discussing
the possibilities of Zen,
the acceptance of everything,
the paradox of burlap
and sainthood.
We decide art
also has its place
in the world,
even as young hoodlums
in hi-tops are clustered
near bushes and trees,
like an exotic species of flora.

It's that kind of day
someone must have already painted,
and we are these two figures
made up of so many
colored dots,
distinguished from the landscape
by an artificial splash
of light.
But don't we really need
to be here like this,
thinking of our fathers,
the tattooed forearm,

W. E. Butts

sure stroke of a cue?
And what about our mothers,
their cumulus lips
floating in the spring air?

Listen friend,
no matter what we make of things,
their details are always hidden,
like the songs
of those nameless birds
we never see.
It's like returning
to the difficult passage
of a book,
or standing in a roomful of flowers
with the body of someone
you might have loved once.
Let's study its pale, folded hands,
the heart gone gray.
Let's study the mysterious trees,
and the impossible names
we give them.

My Father's Name

Twenty years dead, and still Mother
calls me by his name,
which is a river,
ebb of sea marsh,
mussels and kelp.
It is the lesser heron
and least sandpiper.
It is silt and sea grass,
badger and eel.

Say it again,
it becomes waves
repeating themselves
against the pilings.
It is curve of riverbank.
It is the closed factory
and abandoned houses.
It is a gathering of clouds.

My father's name is a bridge
crossing a river
where a man and son fish
near willows bending
over the murky water
like heads hung in prayer,
and light is a sound
only the dead can hear.

W. E. Butts

The Blessing

Standing beneath that blind eye,
the moon,
alone with the wind
and diminishing ships,

I'm watching a gull
drift in the harbor,
pieces of fish
dangling from its beak,
other gulls circling
with sly disinterest,

like when you're a child
pretending not to care
you've been born
into a world
of perennial desire,

as I was when I went, alone,
with fruit to the river,
and lay in my exile of weeds
and croaking frogs.

I don't know what I wanted
that afternoon I was angry
and shouted at Mother.
I remember Father coming
to bring me home—
his low voice,
the dog barking behind him.

Tonight, a ship's horn blares,
the bridge is raised,
those shriveled leaves
floating past the dock
over the quiet waves
repeat his death,
and darkness is a father:

the loudness and silence
of everything.

Saved

My father dealt antiques,
an avocation those times he wasn't
at his factory shift or teaching me,
his only son, some necessary skill
of boyhood—fingers on the seam
of a baseball, earthworm on the hook,
the knife blade slicing away
from my apprenticed hand that gripped
the beginning of something truly made.

People said he had a kind of knack
for recognizing the real value
in the obscure, the worth of wood
beneath aged, peeling paint, the possible
mechanics of those things broken.
And sometimes he'd bring me to that place
of auctioneer's chant and distant past,
mystery of language and the highest bid.

This is where I learned men and women
came to live by code and signal, how
a certain gesture was a promise given,
and wondered who would sit again
at the roll-top desk to turn on the student lamp.
Was there a woman to work the spinning wheel?
Who would gather now at the oak table
to share supper and the day's events?

And when Father and I returned
home with all he could bargain for that day,
there'd be a collection of used books
for me to choose from—Alexandre Dumas,
Zane Gray, Sherlock Holmes, a dime novel—
some adventure that would take a boy
to bed with a flashlight to read
through the late hours under the covers.

W. E. Butts

Clay Street

Here is the street in summer
and the old elm shadowing the house.
At the corner, the home
of a prosperous automobile dealer,
father to my best friend Charles
who later became a cop in the city
we all swore to move to someday.
But just now it almost seemed enough
for us boys to count and name the cars
driving toward the Thruway entrance
at the edge of town, or chase each other
past the overgrown field to the creekbank
and grab sunfish shimmering just beneath
the surface of the shallow, murky water.
Or sometimes the village hall fire alarm
would blare, and if it was evening,
the grocer who lived next door
would rush out to join the volunteers.
Then there were the occasional parades:
beauty queens and fireworks, marching bands
and a soldier returning. Midday, the factory
whistles blew, and men and women filled
the dining car downtown. And maybe
we would leave whoever's front porch
we were gathered on to go and watch
the policeman, sales clerk, garage mechanic,

tool-and-die maker, teacher, mayor, and mailman
hunched over the counter, placing orders
with the waitress with piled-up hair,
who knew them all by name and would,
they were certain, deliver them
their plates of guaranteed homecooking.
Some afternoons, Sammy the junkman
came riding by, his old horse pulling
a cart full of metal scraps and cloth,
and when he cried, "rags"
we'd shout back our senseless taunts,
until he neared the small stone bridge
and the house where two spinster sisters lived
with their bachelor brother who never spoke.
Under that bridge we plotted our futures
of high scores and smiling girls, the secret lives
we believed we would have, and called out
then to the echoing shade.

W. E. Butts

Sunday Factory

We walk the long street
Sunday afternoon,
past the stone church, on our way
to visit his place of work.
This is the religion of father and son,
the faith of a boy who's only five,
the factory a blessing of meat and bread,
the big machines still as statues,
an assembly of clocks
to mark the next week's labor.
Here are the instruments of the makers,
their testaments of gears and wheels.
This is where men and women are called
to the daily stations of common task,
and so I stand with my father
in a child's reverent silence.
Tomorrow, he'll enter the loud,
humming chorus of his eight hour shift
to hose down the conveyor belts
so many times his forearms will ache
until they become light as air.
This is when he thinks of the boy
and his schoolbooks, remembers his wife
and her lilac corsage that morning they married.
And he makes what he can from each of these hours
that will, at last, take him home.

Red Jack

I was twelve that day Father brought me to the home
of his friend, a man living alone, small pension
and afternoons at the window. I remember the percolator's
aroma and dance, a cigar's blue smoke. They sat at the kitchen
table and spoke for a while about the factory closed,
the railroad gone, men they had known lost in the War,
and before that, the Depression and the ten dollar bill
my father left once in his mailbox. And so a boy learned
the tone and gesture of trust and resolve. At my father's wake
seven years later, Red Jack's nephew James stood next to me,
his uncle dead, and we held the silence between us
like a handshake. Once, we had been altar boys,
and served Mass for a priest who kept raising his cup
to the wine cruet, demanding more of Christ's blood,
and when James hid in the sacristy and drank from the rest
until he was sick, I never told. After the funeral, I left town
for college and the decades of mistakes a man can make,
whether he goes away from the place he was born, or not.
James went to work at a local plant, where he lost
two fingers trying to cut metal under a blade
like the older machinists, without using a safety guard.
It was piecework, and he needed the extra money
for the pregnant girlfriend he'd been dating since high school.

W. E. Butts

They married and, when their two kids had grown
and moved on, divorced. He and I still talk, and last night,
on the phone, it was as if the years of failure, faith, confession,
and hope were being emptied into this single moment,
each of us hanging on to the end of the other's line
and the chance to save ourselves, yet again.

The Train

The train arrives
and birds scatter from the dying elm
to accept the field of late autumn grass.
The land extends a distance
that could reveal
some hidden, unknown thing.
But here, my father, a railroad
man's son, steps across
the rusted, weed-filled tracks,
bringing his suitcase of unspoken words.
In the field, the birds forage
insect and seed,
return with cries and questions.
In this dream, I become the ghost
my father was, one man traveling
between small destinations.
He hands me his suitcase,
and waits now as I board the train.
Our face floats through the coach window,
past a sequence of landscapes.
This is America, 1917, the Kaiser "over there";
they've taken German out of the schools,
and I'm left with my one simple language.
It's 1929: Buffalo, New York,
men going over the Falls in a barrel.

W. E. Butts

I meet a boatman in a bar
the night before a long distance swim
and pay him ten dollars.
Next morning, alone on the gray shore of Lake Ontario,
I decide to go on as far as I can.
Years later, half my stomach gone
to ulcers, I study taxidermy,
and am devoted, for a while, to preserving
the small bodies of frightened animals.
But I get a job, third shift,
cleaning the gelatin-filled machines
at the confectionary dessert plant
next to the railroad tracks, where each night
I listen for the steaming engines.
In 1942, I finally marry. Our first child is stillborn,
and the second so ill the doctors aren't sure
he'll survive, but he does.
Five-years-old, I baffle the lifeguards
with my determination to remain underwater.
At school, we have air raid drills,
nuns directing us to shelter and prayer.
Sundays, at church, I kneel with my parents
in silence, while songbirds warble in the rafters.
I'm twelve, at the railyard,
walking the tracks by the coal cars and ash,
kicking gravel into the tunnel's loud darkness.

I can hear a locomotive's whistle,
a diesel's hiss and grind at the crossing,
and Father, we are the trembling earth.

W. E. Butts

Notes

"Black Squirrels" is for Peter Kidd and Richard Blevins

"A Brief History" is for Keith Kuzmak

"Magic Acts" is for James Duffy

"Smoke" was inspired by the 1995 film of the same title, by Wayne Wang and Paul Auster

The lines *Only the dreamer / can change the dream* in "Observance" refer to the title of John Logan's *Selected Poems* (The Ecco Press, 1981)

"Monarch" and "The Question" are for William Kemmett

"Eight Ball" is for Jack Myers

"The Station" is for the Mississippi delta blues musician Big Jack Johnson

"Arboretum" is for Richard Martin

Section IV, *Sunday Factory*, is for my father, Russell M. Butts

About the Author

 W. E. Butts was born and raised in upstate New York. He attended Goddard College and holds an MFA in Writing from Vermont College. He is the author of seven previous poetry collections, including *Movies in a Small Town* (Mellen Poetry Press), which was nominated for the 1997 Jane Kenyon Outstanding Book of the Year Award, and a chapbook, *Sunday Factory*, from Finishing Line Press. He has been nominated for a Pushcart Prize, and received awards from the Massachusetts Artists Foundation and New England Writers. His poems have been published in several magazines and anthologies, including *Atlanta Review, Mid-American Review, Poetry East, The 1997 Anthology of Magazine Verse, Open Door: A Poet Lore Anthology 1980-96, Under the Legislature of Stars: 62 New Hampshire Poets* (Oyster River Press), and *Heartbeat of New England: Contemporary Nature Poetry* (Tiger Moon Press). He has taught in poetry workshops at the University of New Hampshire, and is currently associate professor of English at Hesser College. He lives in Manchester, New Hampshire where, together with his wife, the poet S Stephanie, he edits the literary journal *Crying Sky: Poetry & Conversation*.